ROLLER HOCKEY

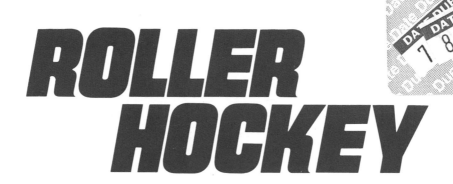

ROLLER HOCKEY

CAM MILLAR

Photographed by Bruce Curtis

Sterling Publishing Co., Inc.
New York

Library of Congress Cataloging-in-Publication Data

Millar, Cam.
    Roller hockey / Cam Millar ; photographed by Bruce Curtis.
        p.   cm.
    Includes index.
    Summary: Covers the equipment, rules, tactics, and powerskating
techniques for roller hockey.
    ISBN 0-8069-4375-0
    1. Roller hockey—Juvenile literature.   [1. Roller hockey.
2. Hockey.]   I. Curtis, Bruce, ill.   II. Title.
GV859.7.M55   1996
796.2′1—dc20   95-39403
                                                                          CIP
                                                                          AC

Designed by Judy Morgan

1   3   5   7   9   10   8   6   4   2

First paperback edition published in 1996 by
Sterling Publishing Company, Inc.
387 Park Avenue South, New York, N.Y. 10016
© 1996 by Cam Millar and Bruce Curtis
Distributed in Canada by Sterling Publishing
℅ Canadian Manda Group, One Atlantic Avenue, Suite 105
Toronto, Ontario, Canada M6K 3E7
Distributed in Great Britain and Europe by Cassell PLC
Wellington House, 125 Strand, London WC2R 0BB, England
Distributed in Australia by Capricorn Link (Australia) Pty Ltd.
P.O. Box 6651, Baulkham Hills, Business Centre, NSW 2153, Australia
Printed and bound in Hong Kong
All rights reserved

Sterling ISBN 0-8069-4375-0 Trade
0-8069-4376-9 Paper

C O N T E N T S

This book is for my Dad, the best coach a kid could ever have. He had me skating at the age of two, and later taught my brother and me to enjoy practising the skills required to play the game of hockey. And best of all, he didn't push either one of us into playing organized hockey (in Canada yet!) until we wanted to play with all our hearts.

ACKNOWLEDGMENTS

This book took the combined and coordinated efforts of many people, all of whom share a love for the game of hockey. Thanks first to photographer Bruce Curtis, who allowed numerous pucks and skates to come flying towards his camera lens!

Special thanks to Ron Kraut, David Berke, and all the players from the Chelsea Piers Roller Hockey and Sky Rink Ice Hockey programs in New York City; Marty Zirpola and all the players from Valley Stream Roller Hockey on Long Island; Joe Delecki from Eastern Ice Sports; and to Concetta Pereira, who, after letting us fill up her family car with hockey equipment and kids, was kind enough to make sure we all had enough food and water to last through a particularly long, hot photo session. Finally, I couldn't have finished this book without Liz Marino's line drawings or Marsha Genensky's efforts to clean up my English.

INTRODUCTION

Fig. 1

Roller hockey is no longer simply a way for ice hockey players to stay in shape during the off season. The game has really come into its own in recent years as a legitimate competitive team sport. Professional roller hockey leagues enjoy major commercial sponsorship and television coverage; new magazines devote themselves entirely to roller hockey; and large amateur organizations have been established to create opportunities to play for enthusiasts of all ages, to sponsor competitions, and to train hockey officials and players.

Roller hockey has become so popular that in some cities in the U.S., more people are registered in roller hockey leagues than in baseball leagues. Is America changing its national game? Even if the answer is no, this exciting new sport is definitely here to stay.

Because roller hockey is so closely related to the game of ice hockey, many of the exercises in this book are similar to ice hockey exercises and concepts. While some translate directly from ice hockey to roller hockey, others must be adapted to the technical demands of in-line skates.

Hockey is a game of instant response and reaction to constantly changing situations. Hockey players must learn to improvise and adjust their thinking every time they step onto the rink. To prepare for the many situations that may arise during the course of a game, study and practise the exercises in this book alone, with a partner, and with your teammates. Work constantly to master the elements of skating, stickhandling, passing, and shooting, and spend time thinking about the game. As you learn to contribute the benefit of your skills to your team, the game will become more enjoyable, and after all, that is the whole point of playing!

This book is intended to be used as a guide for beginning players and as a book of drills and reminders for players with some experience who wish to improve their overall game. It is also written for less experienced roller hockey coaches who want to learn how to teach their players the skills required to play the game.

A complete description of all of the rules of roller hockey is beyond this book, so please check your local hockey league, library, or sporting goods store to find out about amateur league rules for your area.

Fig. 2

Fig. 3

A final note: I have used the terms "he" and "his" throughout the book not to exclude women and girls, but for expediency only. By forbidding body checking, amateur roller hockey rules encourage everyone—women, men, girls, and boys—to participate in the sport. Without the element of body checking, success in the game of roller hockey is a matter of skill and agility rather than brute strength.

chapter one

EQUIPMENT

SKATES

Your skates are your most important pieces of hockey equipment! They must be chosen carefully and must fit properly in order for you to play your best game. Virtually every style, make, or model of in-line skates (except speed skates) is appropriate for roller hockey. Some people prefer to wear the traditional quad roller skate, but in-line skates are better suited for the demands of modern roller hockey.

You should consider several things when choosing your in-line skates:

SKATE STYLE

With increased competition among the major in-line skate manufacturers, there are an amazing number of different skate styles, models, and colors to choose from. Select either skates specifically designed for roller hockey or well-built fitness and recreational skates. The old axiom "You get what you pay for!" applies to in-line skates. Playing roller hockey will really test the strength and durability of your skates.

SKATES FOR BEGINNERS OF ALL AGES

In-line skates designed specifically for roller hockey look similar to ice-hockey skates; and the boots are usually fastened with laces rather than buckles. These boots do not offer enough ankle support for a beginning skater of any age! Most children, and most beginning adults, are better off with an in-line skate with at least one buckle around the ankle. On the other hand, it is essential that you find in-line skates that allow you to bend your ankle!

It is impossible to skate properly wearing skates resembling stiff downhill ski boots! A well-designed fitness or recreational skate offers good lateral ankle support, but allows you to bend your ankle forward.

FOR MORE ADVANCED SKATERS

If you have done some skating and you decide to buy skates with ice hockey–style boots, make sure you take your time and check out all the options. Now that some of the best roller hockey players have given manufacturers the benefit of their experience, the better roller hockey skate manufacturers are making some ice hockey–style lace-up boots with better support through the ankle. Some of these skates are suitable for most other in-line skating activities as well.

Please: Don't take an old pair of ice hockey skate boots and have in-line blades and wheels attached to them unless you are an extremely experienced skater and know exactly what you are looking for! Unless you have played ice hockey for many years, you won't have the proper ankle strength required to play roller hockey in a pair of old, beat-up ice hockey boots!

BOOT FIT

When trying on a pair of skates, make sure you get your heels to the back of the boots. After you fasten the boots, stand up and do some good deep knee bends. Make sure your heels don't slip around. Next, check to see if you can still wiggle your toes while your knees are bent. The boots should offer firm, lateral ankle support, but you should be able to bend your ankles forward with ease.

WHEELS

Playing roller hockey makes special demands on your wheels. The shape, diameter, and hardness of your wheels can have a big effect on your skating. Experience, your skating style, and the type of skating surface you play on most often will help you to decide which wheels suit you best.

Here are some general guidelines for wheels for roller hockey players:

Diameter

Use 70mm–76mm diameter wheels. These wheels will allow you to keep your center of gravity relatively low to the ground and will allow you to get up to full skating speed quickly.

Hardness

The type of surface you play on most often will dictate the hardness of your wheels. Wheels marked "78A" will give you good wear and turning control for almost all surfaces. However, if you plan to play hockey most often on rough concrete or asphalt you should use wheels with a hardness rating of 81A to 88A. Softer wheels will get chewed up very quickly on rough surfaces. If you plan to play hockey most often on smooth concrete, plastic, wood, or painted surfaces, softer wheels, marked from 74A to 80A, will give you more grip and better control in your turns.

Wheel rotation

Learn how to rotate your wheels! You will find that your wheels wear down on the inside edges. Eventually, this will have an adverse effect on your skating and turning, and will destroy your wheels. You can skate more safely, with better technique, and extend the life of your wheels at the same time, by rotating your wheels regularly.

To rotate your wheels, move your front wheel to the rear of your skate. Then move the other wheels forward one space. As you do this, flip each wheel around so that the worn edges face the outside of your boot. Ask a more experienced player to show you how to do this the first time. This will demonstrate that you are serious about the game!

Fig. 4

THE HOCKEY STICK

Your next most important piece of equipment! When selecting a hockey stick, consider the construction of the blade, the curve of the blade, and the height of the stick. If you will be playing outside on rough surfaces, choose a stick with a plastic blade (or one with plastic reinforcement running along the bottom of the blade). If you plan to play on a special plastic or wooden surface, you can use a regular wooden ice hockey stick.

Sticks are usually marked "L" (left) or "R" (right). This refers to the curve of the blade. Don't buy a right curve, or right shot, stick just because you are right-handed! Preference for a right shot stick or a left shot stick is a personal matter, not always related to right-handedness

Fig. 5

or left-handedness. To determine if you are more comfortable carrying a stick with the blade off to your right side or off to your left, pick up a stick and move it around as if you were moving a puck or ball. Keep your hands comfortably apart on the stick. You will quickly discover which hand feels best holding the top of your stick, and which hand feels best for controlling the lower part of the shaft.

STICK LENGTH

The length of your hockey stick is important: if your stick is either too long or too short you will not be able to control the puck or ball. To determine your correct stick length, stand your stick upright on the ground. When you are standing in your skates, the top of the stick should be between your collarbone and your chin. When standing in your street shoes, the stick should be no higher than your mouth. Pencil a mark on the stick and cut it with a saw.

Fig. 6. The proper stick length

Fig. 7

THE PUCK (OR BALL)

The kind of surface you play on will determine whether you should be using a plastic puck or a street hockey ball. On smooth, polished concrete, wooden, or plastic surfaces, you can use a plastic roller hockey puck, designed to emulate an ice hockey puck. On rough concrete or asphalt parking lots, streets, or playgrounds, you are better off with a street hockey ball. A plastic puck won't glide smoothly over rough surfaces; instead, it will take totally unpredictable twists and turns. But a street hockey ball is more predictable on rough surfaces and will allow for a faster game.

TAPING THE END OF THE STICK

Once you have cut your stick to the correct length, put some tape (or secure a pre-formed plastic grip) on the end of the shaft. This will give you a good grip for passing and shooting, and will make it easier for you to pick up your stick if you drop it. Don't overdo it! You don't want your taped stick too awkward to grip.

Fig. 8

Fig. 9

PROTECTIVE EQUIPMENT

It is true that you only need to have in-line skates, a stick, and a puck or ball in order to play roller hockey. But roller hockey is not the same as ice hockey. Playing roller hockey without protective gear is not safe. When you fall on wood, asphalt, or cement without protective gear, you don't slide as you would on ice. If you want to really play roller hockey to the best of your ability—with confidence, speed, and full concentration—you must wear full protective gear. You won't have to worry about losing skin off of your elbows or knees! The game becomes even more fun!

Protective equipment for roller hockey is specially designed with plastic pads that allow you to slide on the ground upon contact. Roller hockey equipment is less expensive than ice hockey equipment; it's also much more lightweight, it's air-breathable, and it allows for full movement of your arms and legs. All the major in-line manufacturers make excellent hockey equipment.

You can wear ice hockey equipment instead of specially designed roller hockey gear. But, because ice hockey equipment was not designed to slide on concrete, you should use your oldest or least wanted ice hockey gear. It will get pretty roughed up.

Always wear elbow pads, shin and knee pads, gloves, and a helmet. Shoulder pads are a good option as well. Most organized roller hockey leagues require players to wear all the above equipment, including a helmet with a full face shield.

Fig. 10. A properly equipped player

ROCKERING YOUR WHEELS

Flat wheels

Most in-line skates come from the factory with flat wheels: all four wheels of each skate touch the ground at the same time.

Rockered wheels

The purpose of rockering your wheels is to emulate the action of ice skates, with their slightly curved blades. With rockered wheels, when the two middle wheels of each skate touch the ground, the front and rear wheels remain slightly off the ground.

Skates with rockered wheels make less contact with the ground; this makes it easier to perform the tight turns and crossovers required in the game of hockey. If your skates can be rockered, you should try them in this position. Some people never go back to flat wheels after skating on rockered wheels!

To learn how to rocker your wheels, refer to the owner's manual for your skates, or ask an experienced skater or skate shop salesperson to show you.

If your skates cannot be rockered, you can create a similar effect by putting slightly smaller wheels in the front and rear positions of your frames. (For example: place 70mm wheels in the front and rear positions, and 72mm wheels in the middle two positions on your skate frames).

chapter two

POWER
SKATING

The most important ingredient in becoming a fine hockey player is skating! If you want to improve your overall hockey game, you must never neglect your skating skills. All professional players work on their skating every day in order to stay in top form, each striving to be the fastest and most agile hockey player his body will allow him to be.

Regardless of whether you are a beginning skater, a good skater who wants learn to play roller hockey, or an experienced hockey player who wants to remain serious about skating, these skating concepts and exercises are essential to power skating practice.

"HOCKEY POSITION"

Here is where all your action begins! From this position you should feel that you are ready to move in any direction. Real power skating requires that you always have your knees bent. You should feel that your knees are centered over the balls of your feet. You can make sure that your knees are adequately bent by letting your ankles lean forward against the tongue of your skates. Use this as a reminder every once in a while to check your knee bend.

Fig. 11. Hockey position—front

Fig. 12. Hockey position—side

FORWARD SKATING

Starting (or "V") position

Once you've established "hockey position," you are ready to move. With your knees bent, point your toes out in "V" position. Make sure your knees are still over your toes and that you feel solidly balanced. Stay centered; don't lean back on your heels.

Fig. 14. "V" position—side view

Fig. 13. "V" position—front view

FORWARD STRIDING

From the starting position, stride forward with your left skate, at the same time giving a push with your right skate (Fig. 15).

Center yourself over your left leg as you begin to bring your right leg forward (Fig. 16).

As you bring your right leg forward, you should be getting ready to give a push with your left skate. Your feet should still be in the turned-out, "V" position (Fig. 17).

As you push with your left skate, stride forward onto your right leg. Center yourself over your right leg while maintaining a good knee bend (Fig. 18).

Now, give a good push with your right skate as you prepare to stride with your left. This cycle of pushing, striding, centering, and bringing the rear leg forward while preparing to push off with the other skate repeats itself again and again (Fig. 19).

Fig. 16

Fig. 15

Fig. 17

Fig. 18

Fig. 19

TIPS FOR FORWARD STRIDING

• Keep your eyes and head up.

• Make sure your knees are always bent, and your center of gravity stays level. Don't bob up and down.

• Feel your shin against the tongue of your skate boot to be sure that you have a good knee bend.

• Don't sit back on your heels. Keep your knees over the balls of your feet.

STRONG INSIDE EDGES

Real skating power is created by the strength with which you push and stroke with what are known as the inside edges of your wheels.

Fig. 20. Push into those inside edges!

THE SWIZZLE

This seemingly simple maneuver is actually a foundation exercise that will almost single-handedly improve all aspects of your skating. Practising the swizzle helps you to feel your inside edges, works on your knee bend, stretches and strengthens your groin and inner thighs, and improves your balance. Start with your knees bent and your skates in the "V" position (Fig. 21).

Push with both inside edges until your feet come to about shoulder-width apart (Fig. 22).

Point your toes inward in order to pull your skates back together (Fig. 23).

Now, with your knees still bent, point your toes out, and push with your inside edges in order to repeat the swizzle (Fig. 24).

Fig. 22

Fig. 21

Fig. 23

Point your right skate inward to finish "carving" the letter "C" (Fig. 27).

Bring your right skate back as close as possible to your left, and bend your knees in preparation for swizzling with your left leg (Fig. 28).

Now push with the inside edge of your left skate. Center your weight over your right leg and hold your right skate in a straight line.

Fig. 24. Finish the swizzle.

ONE-FOOT SWIZZLES ("C" CUTS)

Do this exercise with all your wheels in contact with the ground. Instead of pushing with both skates at the same time, push with one skate while holding the other in a straight line. Think of your inside edges "carving" the letter "C" on the ground. Again, work on bending both knees at all times.

To start off, bend both knees and then turn your right skate out in the "V" position (Fig. 25).

Push with your right inside edge to about shoulder-width apart while staying centered over your left leg and holding your left skate in a straight line (Fig. 26).

Fig. 25

Fig. 26

Fig. 27

Fig. 28

ONE-FOOT SWIZZLING ("C" CUTS) IN A CIRCLE

This exercise will build your strength and balance, and will prepare you to execute great turns and crossovers.

Imagine a circle on the ground (or use a face-off circle drawn on the hockey rink). To move counterclockwise, stand with your left skate on the line of the circle. Turn your right skate out in the "V" position. Turn your head and upper body to the left, center yourself over your left leg as you bend your knees, and prepare to push with your right inside edge (Fig. 29).

Pushing with your right skate, begin to "carve" the letter "C." Stay centered over your left leg and hip, making sure that your left knee is bent. Keep your eyes, head, and upper body rotated to the left (Fig. 30).

Finish "carving" the letter "C" by pointing your right toe inward, and bring your skates back together as close as possible (Fig. 31).

Stay centered over your left leg as you start another swizzle with your right skate. Make sure your knees are bent, and keep looking to the left, across the circle.

Fig. 30

Fig. 29

Fig. 31

TURNING

Unlike stopping on ice skates, it is pretty hard to stop in a split second on in-line skates. Therefore, roller hockey is a game of constant turning. In order to master the game, you have to master turns: tight turns that take you to the puck, quick turns to avoid collisions, and wide turns that get you in the clear for a pass. The ability to turn with control at all speeds will make you valuable to your team and will lessen your chances of injuring yourself or another player.

Here are the rules of turning for roller hockey:

• To turn to the left, roll your left skate forward and turn your eyes, head, upper body, and hips to the left. Keep both skates in contact with the ground! When turning to the right, lead with your right skate and turn your eyes, head, upper body, and hips to the right.

• Let your hockey stick lead you around the turn.

• Keep your knees bent.

• Don't sit back on your rear wheels. Stay centered, and keep your balance over the balls of your feet.

• Learn to trust your wheels to hold you through the turn. Feel the rubber digging into the ground during a tight turn. You are now trusting both your outside and your inside edges. You are on the outside edge of your leading skate, and the inside edge of your trailing skate.

Fig. 32

Fig. 33

Fig. 34. A well-executed turn

Fig. 35. Keep both of those skates on the ground!

STATIONARY CROSSOVERS (WALKOVERS)

This drill should be done before trying front (or back) crossovers. Do these crossovers slowly to begin with. Start with your feet comfortably apart. Transfer your weight to your right hip, and center yourself over your right skate (Fig. 36).

Begin to cross your left skate over the top of your right, pointing your left toe downwards and to the right to help keep your balance over your right hip and skate (Fig. 37).

Land on the ball of your left foot. Shift your weight onto your left hip, and center yourself over your left skate (Fig. 38).

Bring your right skate back alongside the left, and allow your weight to come back to center (Fig. 39).

Now, shift your weight back to the left hip and center yourself over your left skate (Fig. 40).

Pick up your right skate and cross it over the left, pointing the toe of your right skate downwards and to the left. Land on the ball of your right skate. Bring your left skate back alongside your right, and let your weight come back to center.

Fig. 36

Fig. 38

Fig. 37

Fig. 39

Fig. 40

FORWARD CROSSOVERS IN MOTION

After practising one-foot swizzles around a circle and stationary crossovers, you should be ready to try some forward crossovers. Once you have mastered both right-over-left and the left-over-right crossovers, you will be able to maintain speed while turning, and will therefore become a more agile player.

Let's do a right-over-left crossover. While moving counterclockwise around a circle, center your weight over your left, inside leg (Fig. 41).

Pick up your right skate and move it over your left. Keep your upper body rotated to the left, and stay relaxed and centered over your left leg (Fig. 42).

Prepare to land on the ball of your right foot, making

sure that your knees are still bent (Fig. 43).

As you land on your right skate, push through with the outside edge of your left skate (Figs. 44 and 45).

Bring your left skate alongside the right. Start to center yourself over the left hip and skate again in order to execute another crossover.

Fig. 41

Fig. 42

Fig. 43

Fig. 44

Fig. 45

THE CROSSUNDER

The crossunder is the pushing technique used by the inside leg at the end of a crossover.

In our example, the skater is bringing his right, outside skate over his left, inside skate during a counter-clockwise crossover. You can also say that he is crossing his left skate under his right.

As the skater touches down with his right skate, he continues pushing with his left skate (the crossunder skate) until his leg is fully extended.

In the clockwise turn, our skater is pushing with his right skate as he prepares to cross his left skate over his right. With his right skate (now the crossunder skate), he maximizes his push until his right leg is fully extended.

Working on the crossover-crossunder technique will supply you the extra power and speed you need to accelerate out of your turns. Practise slowly and build up speed.

Fig. 47

Fig. 48

Fig. 46

BACKWARD SKATING

You must be able to skate as well backwards as you can skate forward to succeed in the game of roller hockey. Defensemen, especially, must be masters of backward movement, as time and time again during the course of a game they face opposition Forwards, who come at them at full speed. And Forwards must be able to maneuver in every possible direction in order to gain the best scoring positions in the rink.

THE BACKWARD SWIZZLE

This is the best introduction to skating backwards. It is the exact opposite of the forward swizzle.

Start with knees bent and your toes pointed inward (Fig. 49).

Push with the inside edges of both skates, bringing them to about shoulder-width apart. Feel that you are finishing your push by rolling off the balls of your feet (Fig. 50).

Point your heels inward, and pull your skates back together (Fig. 51).

With your knees still bent, point your toes inward as you prepare for another backward swizzle (Fig. 52).

Fig. 49

Fig. 50

Fig. 51

Fig. 52

BACKWARD STOPPING

The backward swizzle is also good practice for coming to a stop while skating backwards. From a backward glide, with legs shoulder-width apart, turn your toes out, and lower your center of gravity so that you are almost in a sitting position. Keep applying pressure to your inside edges as you start to slow yourself down.

Fig. 53

BACKWARD ONE-FOOT SWIZZLES IN A CIRCLE (BACKWARD "C" CUTS)

The ability to move in any direction while skating backwards will help you in defensive situations. It will help you maneuver around the other team's goal when you are trying to get into the open for a pass or shot. This exercise will give you strength and maneuverability while skating backwards.

Imagine a large circle on the ground (or use a face-off circle painted on the rink). To move backwards clockwise, start by standing with your left skate on the line of the circle, with your eyes and head looking back over your left shoulder. As you look over your left shoulder, bend your knees and point the heel of your right skate out, in preparation for a good inside edge push (Fig. 54).

As you push with your right skate to begin to trace the letter "C," stay centered over your left, inside leg. Keep looking over your left shoulder (Fig. 55).

Point your right heel inward (towards your left leg) to bring your right skate back alongside your left. Remain centered over your inside leg (Fig. 56).

With your knees still bent, point your right heel out, and push again with the inside edge of your right skate to start another "C" cut.

Fig. 54

Fig. 55

Fig. 56

BACKWARD CROSSOVERS

Don't neglect your backward skating skills! You're not a complete hockey player until you are just as comfortable skating backwards as you are skating forward. Backward crossovers are not that difficult to learn, provided you have built yourself a solid foundation by having mastered all the previous exercises.

Just as you would in backward one-foot swizzles ("C" cuts), imagine your circle of travel. Practise your backward "C" cuts while moving clockwise in order to get moving. As you are gliding, look over your left shoulder as you center your weight over your inside leg (Fig. 57).

Remain centered over your inside leg as you begin to pick up your right skate. Keep your left knee bent and continue looking over your left shoulder (Fig. 58).

Bring your right skate across the front of your left skate. Keep it low to the ground (Fig. 59).

Land on the ball of your right foot. Center yourself over your right skate as you now prepare to take a large, reaching step with your left skate (Fig. 60).

Keeping your knees well bent in order to maintain a low center of gravity, take a large reaching step with your left skate to move it to the inside of the circle (Fig. 61).

As you land on your left skate, immediately center yourself over your left leg as you prepare for another right-over-left backward crossover (Fig. 62).

Fig. 57

Fig. 59

Fig. 58

Fig. 60

FRONT-TO-BACK TRANSITIONS

Defensemen take note! You must be able to make this move while turning to either side without losing any momentum.

Let's say that you want to make a front-to-back transition while watching out for a player on your right side. Look over your right shoulder as you are skating or gliding. Start to shift your weight to your left hip (Fig. 63).

Center yourself over your left hip as you swing your right skate and shoulder around to the right. This will

Fig. 61

Fig. 63

Fig. 62

cause you to pivot on your left skate (Fig. 64).

Now shift your weight to your right hip as your right skate lands on the ground (Fig. 65).

With your weight centered over your right hip, lift your left skate and plant it securely back on the ground about shoulder-width apart from your right skate (Fig. 66).

Once you have both feet securely on the ground about shoulder-width apart, make sure your knees are bent and you are gliding backwards in a solid, balanced position. You should now feel ready to make a move in any direction (Fig. 67)!

Fig. 65

Fig. 64

Fig. 66

Fig. 67

BACK-TO-FRONT TRANSITIONS

Again, Defensemen take note! This is the move that pays your bills! You have to master this transition to either side. Let's say you want to turn to your right in order to check a player who is racing down the rink.

As you are gliding or skating backwards, look over your right shoulder (in the direction in which you wish to move). This is your most important step (Fig. 68)!

Fig. 68

Center your weight over your left hip as you rotate your whole upper body and head to the right (Fig. 69).

With your weight centered over your left hip, pick up your right skate and start to swing it to the right. By now your upper body should be fully rotated to the right (Fig. 70).

Prepare to give a good push with the inside edge of your left skate (Fig. 71).

As you push with your left skate, stride forward onto your right skate. You are now ready to skate forward as hard as you can (Fig. 72)!

Fig. 70

Fig. 69

Fig. 71

Fig. 72

TIPS FOR BETTER ALL-ROUND SKATING

• Feel that your hips are a focal point of balance and strength.

• Keep your eyes and head up. Feel that your eyes are leading you wherever you want to go.

• Always rotate your upper body in the direction you want to turn.

• Make sure you are bending your knees at all times. See if you can feel the tongue of your skate boots with your lower shins.

Fig. 79

TRAIN ENGINE PUSHES

Again, you need a partner. Find someone about your size. The front skater holds a knee bend down the length of the rink as the rear skater bends his knees, digs in with his inside edges, and pushes on the lower back of his partner. Both skaters should keep their eyes up and look ahead the whole way down the rink.

TURNING ZIGZAGS

Set up a turning course with some cones or markers. Start at one end of the rink and see how quickly you can make it to the other end. Remember to keep both skates on the ground and both hands on your stick throughout the turn and to keep rotating your upper body in the direction you want to go.

Fig. 80

FAST BREAKS ON THE WHISTLE

Line up at one end of the rink. When the coach or a friend blows the whistle, break for the other end of the rink as fast as possible, holding your stick with your top hand. This will improve your reaction time and get your fast skating muscles in shape.

All roller hockey players must work hard at avoiding "one-speed" skating, or "slow-twitch-muscle-only" skating. With the constant circling and turning involved in roller hockey, it is easy to become lazy. You will only develop the quick muscle response needed for the really fast, quick break-out style of skating needed to play the game if you really push yourself and work at skating as fast as you can.

Fig. 81

chapter four

STOPPING

It is best to learn how to play roller hockey without having to rely on the traditional heel braking system. There are two reasons not to use a heel brake when playing hockey:

• During play, a sudden stop using the heel brake can cause you to lean backwards, setting you up for a backward fall.

• Stopping with your weight on your heels puts you in an awkward position for handling the puck, and makes it difficult and slow to get back into the play.

In preparation for playing roller hockey, you should learn how to stop in several different ways.

THE SNOWPLOW

Similar to the swizzle, this method should be used to slow yourself down or come to a stop from a very low speed. Point your toes inward and apply pressure to the inside edges of your wheels. Keep your knees bent and lower your center of gravity (Fig. 82).

THE T-STOP

Again, this method should be used to slow yourself down, or to come to a stop from a lower speed. As you lunge forward onto one leg, drag the inside edges of all four wheels of your rear skate. Keep applying pressure with those inside edges as you shift your weight onto your front leg (Fig. 83).

Fig. 82

Fig. 83

THE POWER SLIDE (OR TIGHT-TURN STOP)

This is the most practical method of stopping for roller hockey players. Before trying this method, you should be comfortable making tight turns with both feet on the ground, but you shouldn't be surprised if you fall during your first attempts.

In order to make a power slide, begin as if you are making a tight turn, but rather than rotating your upper body, keep it focused straight ahead.

Let's say you are going to power slide by turning to your left with your right leg extended. From a glide, enter into a tight turn to the left. Really bend the knee of your left leg in order to lower your center of gravity. Don't rotate your upper body to the left; focus straight ahead.

Bring your right leg in front of you in the direction of your stop, and feel the inside edges of your right wheels or the boot itself skid along the ground. Keep applying pressure onto those inside edges. Remember to stay low!

Fig. 84

THE HOCKEY STOP

This method of stopping should only be attempted once you have mastered the power slide. Let's do a hockey stop with the right leg extended.

Skate or glide into a turn as in the power slide. Focus your body straight ahead as both skates turn to the left, and then lower yourself while turning your hips to the right. Bend your right knee deeply as you lower yourself and begin to take all of your weight on your right skate. Your left skate should be raised slightly off the ground. Because you have lowered your center of gravity, you will be able to safely slide on the inside edges of your right skate wheels. Stay low!

Now, bring your left skate down alongside your right skate. Keep both knees well bent as both skates skid along the ground. Stay well down until you have come to a complete stop! NEVER, never straighten your legs at all during a hockey stop!

Fig. 85

Fig. 86

chapter five

STICKHANDLING

After skating, handling the puck is the most important part of the game. When you have control of the puck, you are in control of the game. The art of stickhandling must never be neglected and should be practised regularly.

GRIP

Your top hand—your control hand—should be placed around the taped top of the stick; your lower hand—your power hand—should hold the shaft of the stick 6 to 12 inches below. Don't put a stranglehold grip on your stick! You have to be able to feel what is happening through your hands. Stay relaxed, with a comfortable but firm grip on the stick. Keep your top elbow away from your upper body.

SIDE-TO-SIDE STICKHANDLING

This is the basis of all stickhandling. You should practise side-to-side stickhandling until you can do it in your sleep. If you use a right-shot stick, place a puck off to the right side of your body. Get into hockey position. Your knees should be bent with feet placed about shoulder-width apart. Place your stick to the right of the puck, and "cup" it as in the photo with what is called the forehand side of the stick.

Sweep the puck in front of you, catch it, and "cup" it with what is called the backhand side of the stick.

Keep moving the puck back and forth in this manner. Stay relaxed with your knees bent, and get in the habit of lifting your eyes and looking away from the puck every once in a while.

Fig. 87

Fig. 88

FRONT-TO-BACK STICKHANDLING

This method of stickhandling will help you set up passes and shots and will help you keep the puck away from the other team as you are carrying it down the rink. If you use a right-shot stick, place the puck off to your right side, also known as your shooting side. Place the blade of your stick behind the puck.

Sweep the puck forward, catching it and cupping it when it is in front of you. Continue stickhandling front to back and back to front.

Fig. 90

Fig. 89

LETTING GO OF YOUR BOTTOM HAND

The ability to handle the stick with your top hand is one of the most important skills in hockey. This skill is useful when you want to create some distance between the puck and an attacking player. You will also become much better at handling the puck while skating backwards when you know that you can hang on to the puck while controlling the stick with your top hand. This drill will really help to strengthen your arms and wrists as well.

Start to practise this move by placing a puck off to your shooting side. Begin by holding the stick with both hands.

As you sweep the puck to one side in front of you, take your lower hand off the stick, and prepare to catch and cup the puck while holding the stick with your top hand alone. Sweep the puck back to the other side in front of you, still holding the stick with your top hand alone.

Fig. 91

Fig. 92

STICKHANDLING WHILE SKATING

Get used to holding on to your stick with both hands when you are skating down the rink. This way, you are always ready to make a pass or take a shot. Keep your eyes and head up and look around for your teammates and for opposition players as well.

Fig. 93

PUSHING THE PUCK AHEAD

When you have the puck and you want to make a fast break down the rink, you are best off pushing the puck ahead of you while controlling your stick with your top hand. With one hand free, you will be able to get more power into your skating as you are accelerating down the rink.

Practise sprinting up and down the rink while pushing the puck in front of you.

Fig. 94

STICKHANDLING AROUND CONES

This is an excellent team or individual drill. You should try placing cones in various setups so you are forced to carry the puck in every possible direction.

Don't overskate the puck. The name of the game is control! Start slow and controlled, and then build up your speed using various cone arrangements.

Fig. 95

STICKHANDLING WITH YOUR FEET

During the course of a game, you will often find the puck under your skates. You may have just checked the puck away from an opponent; you may have just lost the puck while stickhandling; or else a teammate may have attempted to make a pass to you that wasn't quite on your stick. In any case, you should practise moving the puck around with your feet so you will know what to do when these situations arise.

Practise, practise, and practise stickhandling while skating. Stickhandling, after skating, is your most important skill!

Fig. 96

chapter six

PASSING

The fastest way to move the puck from one end of the rink to the other in order to set up a shot on the other team's goal is to pass it from one teammate to the next. A well-executed pass will send the puck across the rink much faster than anybody will ever be able to skate. Passing is an art, but it has to be practised.

THE FOREHAND PASS

You have to learn how to make a great forehand pass without slapping at the puck. A great pass consists of three parts:

• the sweeping of the puck towards your target

• the release of the puck

• the follow-through towards your target

THE SWEEP

First, know where you want to send the puck! Start with the puck on your shooting side, placed near your back foot. Begin to sweep the puck towards your intended target. As you sweep, begin to shift your weight onto your front leg, just as you would when throwing a ball.

THE RELEASE

As you finish sweeping the puck towards your target, keep your stick fairly low to the ground. As you begin to release the puck, most of your weight should be on your front leg. Feel that you are using not just your arms but your entire upper body to make the pass.

Fig. 97

Fig. 98

THE FOLLOW-THROUGH

Keep your eye on your intended target! Follow through with the blade of your stick just as you would follow through with your arm after throwing a ball.

RECEIVING A PASS

Learning how to receive a pass is also an art that has to be practised. You have to learn how to receive hard passes and how to pick up soft passes.

When receiving a pass, don't attack the puck with your blade. Instead, let the puck come to you. Cradle or cup the puck with the blade of your stick and give a little when the puck hits your blade.

Practise the forehand pass with a partner. Stand directly opposite each other so you can follow through correctly with your sticks and upper bodies.

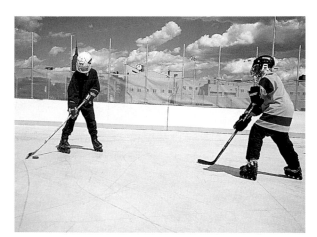

Fig. 100

Fig. 99

THE BACKHAND PASS

Passing with the back side of your stick is called passing off of the backhand side. Backhand passes can be used as a secret weapon to fool the opposition. Once you've mastered backhand passes, you will be able to pass to either side without giving the other team a hint as to where you are going to pass. If you rely on your forehand pass alone, you not only miss out on setting up many scoring opportunities for your team, but the other team can always predict where you will pass.

When practising the backhand pass, set up opposite your partner, just as you would for forehand passing practice, but this time start to sweep the puck with the back side of your blade. Be sure to follow through just as you would in a good forehand pass.

Fig. 101

LEADING THE PASS RECEIVER

The hockey player who passes the puck to a moving teammate in hockey is very similar to the quarterback who throws the football to an intended receiver as he sees him running down the field. You have to anticipate where your teammate will be as you make a pass or throw a ball to somebody in motion. In hockey, you can't just pass the puck to where your teammate is now, because in the second or two it takes you to make the pass, he is going to be further down the rink than he was at the moment you decided to make the pass.

Practise skating up and down the rink making passes back and forth with a partner. Each of you should try to pass the puck to a point in front of the other. Start closely together, and begin at a moderate speed. You can build up the speed when each of you can successfully anticipate the other's movements.

Trade sides so you get practice on the backhand side of your sticks as well as on the forehand side.

Fig. 102

USING THE BOARDS TO MAKE A PASS

Making a pass off the boards (a bank shot) to a teammate will open up many breakout plays from your end of the rink, and will create many scoring opportunities at the other end of the rink as well.

Practise banking the puck off the boards with a partner, varying the distance between you, and practising both forehand and backhand passes.

Fig. 104

PASSING AROUND
THE SQUARE

Set up with your teammates as shown. Get yourselves in hockey position, and pass around the square with full control. Don't let yourselves get sloppy or it will show when you get into a real game. Start slowly and build up the speed of your passing. Stay alert and keep the blades of your sticks on the ground so each passer has a target!

Fig. 105

chapter seven

SHOOTING

There's a simple saying in hockey: "You can't score if you can't get a shot on the net!" The great scorers are constantly working on improving their shooting ability.

THE WRIST SHOT

The term "wrist shot" is actually quite misleading. A good wrist shot requires you to use your whole body, not only your wrists, to get power into the shot!

In any case, this is the most important shot to learn. A good wrist shot is the most accurate shot for most players; it is also a solid foundation for all the other types of shooting. Practising this shot will give you great arm and wrist strength and will also help you become a better passer.

Start the wrist shot just as you would start a good forehand pass. Place the puck back by your rear leg as you stand perpendicular to your intended target. Place most of your weight on your rear leg. Feel as if you are getting set to give a powerful push with your rear leg. Your whole body is going to get into the wrist shot.

Begin to transfer your weight and power to your front leg as you sweep the puck forward. Feel your whole body getting into the shot as you sweep the puck forward. Start to lift your head so you can see your target.

Try to coordinate the release of the puck with the transfer of weight and power to your front leg. Your arms and wrists now give an extra snap as you release the puck. But the shot isn't over yet. You must follow through towards your intended target with your stick. Follow through low for a low shot, and follow through high for a high shot.

Fig. 106

Fig. 107

Fig. 108

your target, snap your lower wrist under as you snap your upper wrist towards you.

Both wrist movements are valid ways to release the puck. While one method may work better for you than the other, it is best to master both. The ability to shoot the puck in different ways will get you more goals.

Fig. 109. The heel of the blade towards the target

DETAIL ON THE WRIST MOVEMENT

At the end of the wrist shot, your wrists give an extra snap to give extra power to the shot. A strong wrist movement also helps to raise the puck off the ground.

When you release the puck in a wrist shot, you can either follow through by pointing at the target with the toe of the blade (the tip of the blade), or by pointing at the target with the heel of the blade (where the blade is joined to the shaft of the stick).

Both types of follow-through require a quick, strong, and definite wrist action from both hands on the stick. To follow through with the toe of the blade pointing at your target, snap your lower wrist over as you snap your top wrist under.

To follow through with the heel of the stick pointing at

Fig. 110. The toe of the blade towards the target

THE BACKHAND SHOT

Wayne Gretzky, the great ice hockey player and all-time leading goal scorer in the NHL, has scored some of his most important record-setting goals using his backhand shot. It's another good secret weapon to have at your disposal.

This shot is similar to a backhand pass, except that you must get your upper body and legs into the shot, just as you do when making a forward wrist shot.

Stand sideways to your intended target. Start with the puck back by your rear leg. Feel yourself getting set to transfer your power and weight onto your front leg.

As you sweep the puck forward, start to transfer your weight onto your front leg and feel that you are really getting your upper body behind the shot.

Just as in a good wrist shot, you must follow through! You can use your wrist snap at the release to raise the puck off the ground.

Fig. 111

Fig. 112

Fig. 113

strike the ground a little behind the puck. This will momentarily slow the stick down and build up a flex in the shaft of the stick as you strike the ground. This built-up flexing in the shaft will act like an extra spring and will help to give more power to your shot.

As you strike the ground with your stick, swing right through the puck, and stay down in order to keep the momentum going. Feel extra power through your hips and legs.

Now, as in the wrist and backhand shots, follow through to keep the momentum going, as well as to determine whether you are going to have a high or low shot. Follow through high for a high shot, and low for a low shot.

Fig. 114

THE SLAP SHOT

This is probably the most glamorous shot in the game, but most goalies love the slap shot because they can see you setting up for it a mile away. It also tends to be the least accurate means of shooting for most players! The slap shot takes a lot of practice and coordination, so don't be disappointed if you haven't got an instantly amazing slap shot. Be patient!

Stand sideways to your intended target. Place the puck between your skates, not too far forward. Start to bring your stick back and transfer most of your weight onto your back leg. As you do so, slide your lower hand a little farther down the shaft of your stick.

Start your downswing with the feeling that most of your power is in your hips and legs. Keeping your eyes on the puck, begin to shift your weight onto your front leg.

Where you make contact with the ground and puck with your stick will help make a good slap shot. Try to

Fig. 115

Fig. 116

Fig. 117

Fig. 118

THE SNAP SHOT

This is one of the most useful shots in hockey. Harder than a wrist shot and more accurate than a slap shot, the snap shot is really a combination of both.

Start the snap shot just as you would start a wrist shot. Sweep the puck forward, but when the puck gets midway between your skates, lift the blade of the stick off the ground just a few inches. You are going to do a mini slap shot.

After you have interrupted your wrist shot, start to transfer your weight onto your front leg. Bring your blade into contact with the puck, at the same time giving a snap with your wrists so that the toe of your blade points towards your intended target.

And now, just as in every other shot, you must follow through! If you've been looking at your intended target, the chances are that you will have a pretty accurate snap shot.

Fig. 119

Fig. 120

Fig. 121

chapter eight

PLAYING THE GAME!

Fig. 131. Notice what the other goalie is doing!

Fig. 132. Shoot low or pass

The "deke"

The art of faking a goalie out of position is called "deking" the goalie. If you have the puck and are coming in on the opponents' goalie on a breakaway, don't just shoot the puck. That makes life all too easy for a goalie. They'd much rather have you shoot at them than "deke" them.

As you break in on the goalie, give a bit of a shoulder and eye fake to one side. You want to make the goalie think that you are going to make a move in that direction.

If the goalie thinks that you are going to cut to your fake side, he will start to slide across his team's net. As soon as you see that he going for your fake, turn and pull the puck back sharply in the other direction.

If the goalie goes for the fake, he will be hopelessly out of position. All you need to do is slide the puck into the open net!

Fig. 133

Fig. 134

Fig. 135

THE DEFENSIVE GAME

The poke check

Your stick isn't only used for passing and scoring! You can take the puck away from an opponent with a fast poke check with the blade of your stick. This skill is essential for all players; Defensemen especially must master the poke check while skating backwards (Fig. 136).

Fig. 136

The stick lift

This is one of the best ways to surprise an opponent and steal the puck. You can do this while coming up from behind or alongside an opponent who has the puck. You don't have to lift the stick very high, but make certain you are strong and sure with your check (Fig. 137).

One on one

When you are the last person between your goalie and the puck carrier, remember the following points:

Fig. 137

• You want to try to force the puck carrier off to one side or the other so he can't get a good shot on the net. Don't get mesmerized by the puck! Look at the chest of the puck carrier. If you watch his body, rather than the puck, then you can anticipate where the puck carrier is going to move. Be prepared to turn from back to front as quickly as you can without taking your eyes off the player with the puck (Fig. 138).

• Don't back in too closely on your goaltender. Make sure he can see the puck at all times.

• Try to make the puck carrier take his shot from a bad angle to the goal. Your goalie will have an easy time stopping a shot from a bad angle.

• Try to poke check the puck carrier. Keep your top arm bent and ready to extend quickly at all times.

Fig. 138. One on one

Two on one

When faced with two opponents coming down the rink towards you, stay between the opponents and don't let one of them get behind you or between you and your goalie (Figs. 139 and 140).

As you get in closer to your own goalie, try to force one of your opponents to take a shot on the goal from a bad angle. At this point, there are two possible outcomes: either the opponent with the puck will take a shot or he will pass to another opponent. While your goalie is worrying about a possible shot, keep your eye on the other player, who may be moving in to take a pass. Stay alert!

Listen to your coach!

Rule number one in organized hockey: "Listen to your coach!" The best teams and players in the world all have coaches. Remember: you're part of a team. Hockey is a game in which you all have to work together in order to win. When you come back to the bench to rest, the game is still going on. Your coach is there to correct mistakes that he has seen during play, to make suggestions to players on some of the finer points of the game, and to help a group of individuals function as a team (Fig. 142).

Drink lots of liquids!

Be sure to keep your energy level high by drinking lots of liquids. Stick to water, fruit juice, or one of the special fluids that are mixed expressly for use by athletes (Fig. 141). Remember to come off the rink for a rest when you are tired. That's why you have teammates!

Fig. 139. Two on one.

Fig. 140. Stay between your opponents.

Fig. 141. Drink lots of liquids.

Fig. 142. Listen to your coach.

chapter nine

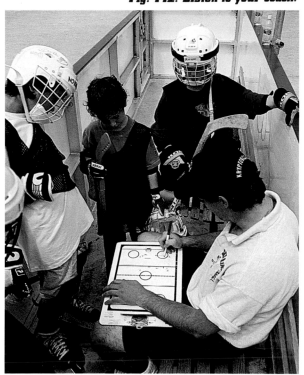

GOALTENDING

Goaltending is another special art form. Even though the goalie is not always involved in the action, he must be focused on the game at all times, ready at all times to make quick, instinctive moves using an entirely different set of skills from those required of his teammates, while wearing the bulkiest equipment on the rink.

EQUIPMENT

A goalie requires special pads and blockers. These include leg pads, a catching mitt, a blocking glove (with which he holds the stick), a helmet with a special goalie's face mask, and chest and upper-arm protection. (Beginners can substitute a regular player's helmet and face shield. But use a real goalie's helmet and mask if you are playing with people who can fire the puck at moderate to high speeds.)

Fig. 144

Fig. 143

PLAYING THE ANGLES

This is the most important concept for a goalie. Suppose you are facing an opposing player who has the puck, and he is getting ready to shoot at you.

If you stand right on the goal line between the goal posts, there is quite a lot of open space into which the shooter can fire the puck. See how much net you are leaving open.

But if you stand farther out from the goal line, you cut down on the possible scoring areas. See how the goalie fills up the net as he moves out towards the shooter.

Moving out from the goal like this is often referred to as "challenging the shooter." The goalie can often force the opposing player to either make a shot or move to a more awkward scoring position.

Fig. 145

Fig. 146

MAKING THE SAVE

Glove saves

Keep your eye on the puck all the way to the net! Once you make the catch, guard the puck so that an opponent doesn't tap it loose for a possible rebound.

Pad saves

Keep your leg pad flush to the ice. You will discover why most goaltenders do their stretching exercises every day! Be prepared to get back up on your feet as quickly as possible.

Skate saves

A goalie must be able to roll out either skate to make these saves. Have your teammates practise shooting low ground shots at you so you can practise quickening your reflexes.

Fig. 147. Glove saves

Fig. 148. Pad saves

Fig. 149. Skate saves

HUG THE GOALPOSTS

When you see an opponent coming around from behind the net with the puck, make sure you are hugging the goalpost so that he can't stuff the puck in the net between you and the goalpost.

COVER THE LOOSE PUCK

If the puck is bouncing around wildly in front of you, pounce on it! Hold the puck for a face-off instead of risking the other team getting to it first.

PASS TO TEAMMATES

Once in a while you will have enough time to make a pass to one of your teammates. This will often surprise your opponents; you can trap them down in your end as you fire the puck up the rink to give your teammates a fast breakout out of your own end.

A warning: be sure and strong with your pass. Otherwise, you will be badly out of position if the other team gets to the puck first.

SPECIAL NOTES FOR GOALTENDERS

The goalie has the most challenging position on the team. As goalie you will be able to stop many shots on the goal, but no matter how good you are, some shots will get by you. Don't get down on yourself when it happens—it's just part of the game.

You may frequently feel all alone in front of your net; but of all the players, the goalie has the best view of the action on the rink. Take advantage of your position. During the game, help inform your teammates about unchecked opponents they may not see. After the game, your observations will be extremely valuable to the other players on your team.

Fig. 150. Hug the goalposts!

Fig. 151. Cover the loose puck!

Fig. 152. Pass to teammates!

INDEX